I0202360

From "The Light" It Flows

Mridula K R

BookLeaf
Publishing

India | USA | UK

Copyright © Mridula K R
All Rights Reserved.

This book has been self-published with all reasonable efforts taken to make the material error-free by the author. No part of this book shall be used, reproduced in any manner whatsoever without written permission from the author, except in the case of brief quotations embodied in critical articles and reviews.

The Author of this book is solely responsible and liable for its content including but not limited to the views, representations, descriptions, statements, information, opinions, and references ["Content"]. The Content of this book shall not constitute or be construed or deemed to reflect the opinion or expression of the Publisher or Editor. Neither the Publisher nor Editor endorse or approve the Content of this book or guarantee the reliability, accuracy, or completeness of the Content published herein and do not make any representations or warranties of any kind, express or implied, including but not limited to the implied warranties of merchantability, fitness for a particular purpose.

The Publisher and Editor shall not be liable whatsoever...

Made with ❤ on the BookLeaf Publishing Platform
www.bookleafpub.in
www.bookleafpub.com

Dedication

Lovingly and respectfully dedicated to my Guru , my divine parents

Late **K.Ravindran** ,Neeravil,Perinad P. O ,Kollam (S/o Late Kumara Panicker ,Kavadivila ,Kollam and

Late Lekshmi,Vilayil house ,Kollam) &Late **KamalaBai** (D/o of Late Narayanan (Njavarakkal ,Puthupally,Kayamkulam and Meenakshi, Padikkathra,Kayamkulam).

Special mention -Our Daughter ,*Ms.Abhirami,K.A* ,who always enlightens me with her divine wisdom inherited from my parents and continues as a permanent source of inspiration and insight to me.

(**cover design :courtesy-Ms.Abhirami.K.A**)

Last , but not the Least to **God's Love**, the only source of ink to my pen.

Dedication

Preface

Everything originates from the source of **Light,** which can be interpreted as a symbol of divine energy, love, or consciousness.

The Light represents the infinite potential, the spark of creation, and the essence of life. From this light, everything flows, implying that all existence, energy, and experiences emanate from this source. It is a reminder of our connection to
the divine, and the idea that we are all part of a larger, interconnected whole.

All 21 poems are expressions of the idea that our lives, relationships, and experiences are all connected to and **flow** from this divine source of **Light.**

From the Light it flows, a river of Love,
Connecting us all, sent from Above.
In its Warmth, we find our Peaceful Nest,
A sense of unity, and eternal Rest.

In this Light, we see the Beauty Rare,
A reflection of the Divine, that's always There.

May we cherish, and honor this sacred Flow,
And spread the Love, that from the Light it Grow

Acknowledgements

To my beloved husband ,Mr.Ajayakumar.K.R

1.My Mother - The Eternal Truth-The Goddess

Mother's warmth, a bliss so sweet,
Everlasting love, our hearts to greet.
Fortune smiles, where her stories unfold,
Precise affection, young and old.

In musical notes of her gentle say,
Life's wisest skills weave a loving way.
No secret hides from her knowing eyes,
Sorrows unknown, like pain that won't demise.

Conflicts unresolved in her loving court,
Remain unsettled, till harmony's sought.
Joy not shared with her, fades like morning dew,
A heart that ignores her grief, isn't true.

Rain that doesn't soothe her tender heart,
Burns the world apart.
Mother's tears like fiery drops descend,
Hot breath of earth, a scorching trend.

Oh humans, transform deeds dark to light,
Let virtues bloom, and wrongs take flight.
May Mother's lullaby rhythm forever flow,

As life's sweet melody, where love does grow.

In her love and shelter, children find delight,
Eating, sleeping, waking, bathed in warmth bright.
Mother's wellness, happiness, health we adore,
Our foremost goal, forevermore.

Let nature's peace and prosperity reign,
Like "Bhoopala Raga", auspiciousness sustain.
In Mother's eternal truth, we find our nest,
Love's haven where hearts find peace and rest.

With Love to Eternal Mother -Mridula

2. My Father, My Guiding Light

A luminary, a guiding light,
You shine so bright, a beacon in the night.
Your love, a treasure trove, a sanctuary true,
A haven where hearts find solace, and dreams come anew.

With wisdom's gaze, you watched us grow,
A sage, a mentor, a friend to know.
Your footsteps marked with kindness and care,
Left an indelible mark, beyond compare.

Your words, a balm to soothe the soul,
A gentle breeze that calms life's turmoil whole.
Your presence, a shelter from life's stormy night,
A safe haven where love and peace take flight.

In your eyes, a deep affection shines,
A love that's pure, a heart that truly mines.
Your touch, a warmth that never fades,
A memory that time cannot erase or shade.

As I grow, I realize your guidance and might,
Shaped me into who I am, a reflection of your light.

I'm grateful for the lessons you taught,
For the love you shared, and the values you've brought.

Though you've moved on, your legacy remains,
A legacy of love, a treasure that sustains.
In my heart, your memory stays,
A guiding force, a love that never fades away.

In Ever Loving Memories of My Father -Mridula

3.Cheish each Moment - Grace The 'Time God '

Time, the master of fate,
Decides what stays, what waits,
What proceeds, what recedes,
What blooms, what withers, what succeeds.

It teaches us to relish the moment,
To let go of what's meant to perish,
To keep some things close to heart,
And leave others to depart.

Time shows us how to evolve,
To revolve, resolve, and dissolve,
To refine and define our path,
And reap the benefits of every aftermath.

The Teacher of all seasons,
Guiding just to live, love, and reason,
To wind up with wisdom and peace,
And respect the clock that never ceases.

Oh, dear ones, learn to cherish Time,
The divine force that shapes our prime,

For in its rhythm, we find our way,
And in its grace, a brighter day.

Cherishing each moment of grace of God -Mridula

4.Fire and The Fire

 A Guru's spark ignites the flame,
Of knowledge, guiding disciples' frame,
Thapsakti's fire, a protective might,
Illuminating paths, banishing endless night.
The agnikund's sacred blaze ascends,
Purifying air, where hearts and minds transcend,
A kindled lamp, a gentle, warming light,
Enlightening countless souls, in its radiant sight.
Yet, wildfire's fury, uncontrolled and free,
Destroys all in its path, a calamity,
The fire's essence remains, pure and divine,
Conditioned, it shines, a beacon sublime.
Like the sun, a fire that lights the day,
Illuminating worlds, in a celestial way,
So too, the fire within, a spark divine,
Condition, polish, protect, and let it shine.
Let your soul emerge, a lighthouse tall,
Protecting, soothing, energizing all,
Enthuse light, ignite the inner spark,
And let your heart illuminate the world's dark.

Light The Fire With Love - Mridula

5.I belong to Him

I belong to Him
I am not a show piece ,
To be displayed in house or public,
Not an object without senses, emotions,
To remain without originality of where I belongs
To remain expressionless for the sarcasm,
Negativity, reflections ,drama, maya around,
Letting them to value me as they wish.

I am not a "jad" attracting only sympathy,
Act of mercy and to burry deep ,being of no use
I am a living being , a human being,
With emotions, values, opinions ,thoughts,
With "five" senses interacting and perceiving
A human with spark of His Light inside,
A miniscule element of His vast Universe
An integral part of Him, His Creation and His material

I belong to Him, emerge from Him and dissolve in Him
A never ending cycle of life and dissolution
Where I have to attain wisdom to reach His Feet
And be with Him permanently
Do allow me to emerge with respect,
Dignity, value , wisdom ,love and empathy

Let me be with His ocean of love and Bliss always
Yes , I belong to Him, the same way all "charachara"

I Surrender myself to Him, the Ultimate Being
The ever pervading "Sarvatman",The Lord Krishna.

Forever devoted to My Lord-Mridula

6.Love and the Lord

Where love resides, there's no weight to bear
No stress, no strain, no anxious care
For love and trust entwined, a perfect pair
But when love's lacking, stress starts to share

Love's not a deal, nor a transaction cold
True love's unconditional, forever to hold
It flows like nature, pure and free
Unfettered by expectations, wild and carefree

The sun shines bright, without a plea
The moon glows soft, in serenity
The sky's vast expanse, a wondrous sight
Rain nourishes, without asking for delight

Soil gives life, without condition or pride
Nature's love, a gift, always at its stride
Don't wait for love, or respect, or care
For true love flows, without expectation or snare

Where there's smoke, fire's often near
Anger, hatred, greed, and ego, bring fear
But fix your mind, on God's unconditional love
The foundation strong, sent from above

In every relationship, a guiding light
Unconditional love, shines through the night
May your heart be filled, with love's pure grace
And may you radiate, love's warm, gentle pace.

Love the Lord- Mridula

7.Life -A Poem written with God's Pen

Life is like a poem written with God' pen
Every stanza written in His language
He only can decode the meaning of each decipher
We have to attain His wisdom to know its meaning
The one who knows about its Author
Understand the meaning of Life,
Each word in the poem stands for.
Those decipher it ,who reside close to His Heart
Those enjoy its melody , who understand His Raga
Who imbibes its "Thala", immerse in its beauty
Who enjoys the beats, sings with its "sruthy"

Love the Life -Mridula

8.Time-The Decision Maker

Time decides everything,
What to reside,
What to recede,
What to proceed,
What to relish,
What to perish,
What to keep beside,
What to keep inside,
What to leave outside,
What to bounce,
What to pounce,
What to enjoy,
What to engulf,
What to change,
What to remember,
What to forgive,
What to live ,
What to leave ,
How to evolve,
Revolve and resolve,
Refine and define us.
Reap benefit of "The Time" ,
The teacher who teaches everything,
How to live, love and "wind up" too,

Learn to respect "Time' ,The God' ,
He surely showers His Grace on Us.

With Love & Respect to Time -Mridula

9.Kindle the Divine spark in His Kindness

Fire, a symbol of knowledge and might,
Ignites the flame of wisdom, shining bright.
The Fire ,Guru's guidance protects and blesses,
Disciples walk the path, their hearts caressing.

The lamp of knowledge dispels darkness around,
Agnikund's sacred fire purifies the ground.
Controlled fire brings warmth and light,
Illuminating minds, banishing endless night.

Like the sun, conditioned fire shines bright,
Illuminating the world, a wondrous sight.
But wildfire's fury, uncontrolled and free,
Destroys all in its path, a calamity.

The fire within you, a spark divine,
Polished and protected, it can shine.
Condition it with wisdom, cherish its might,
And let your soul emerge, a beacon in the night.

Like a lighthouse, guiding ships to shore,
Your inner fire can illuminate more.
Protect, soothe, energize, and enlighten all,

Let your soul's spark ignite, and never fall.

Enjoying the divine spark -Mridula

10.She is My Daughter

She's my guiding star, my shining light,
A beacon on my path, through day and night.
Her presence fills my heart with love and peace,
A treasure given, a precious release.

With words so gentle, yet strong and wise,
She fills my life with joy, and opens my eyes.
A divine flower, spreading love and care,
A golden lamp, that shines with beauty rare.

In her, I see a reflection of God's love,
A blessing sent, from above.
I'm grateful for her presence, every day,
A star that shines, in a loving way.

With no complaints, no sorrow, no pain,
She supports me, and eases my strain.
Together we sing, a duet so sweet,
In perfect harmony, our hearts meet.

She's my daughter, and my guiding friend,
A treasure rare, that never ends.
May God grant her, eternal love and light,
And fill her life, with joy and delight.

Your creations, oh God, are truly grand,
A symphony, of love, in this land.
May we cherish, and honor them with care,
And spread the love, that's always there.

With Everlasting Love to Our Daughter-Mridula

11.Her perception -her father's reflection

In her eyes, a wonder to behold,
A reflection of her Father's soul, so bold.
She tries to mimic his gentle expression,
A painting of love, a divine obsession.

With every glance, she's trying to see,
The world through her Father's eyes, wild and free.
His words are music, his presence a breeze,
That awakens her soul, and brings her to her knees.

In her Father's world, she's found her own,
A universe of love, where she's never alone.
His love is an ocean, deep and wide,
A flame that burns bright, guiding her inside.

With every step, she's trying to understand,
The mysteries of life, and her Father's plan.
She sees the world through his eyes of wisdom,
And finds the truth, that sets her spirit free from.

In her Father's presence, she's home at last,
A sense of peace, that will forever last.
His love is her shelter, her guiding light,

That shines so bright, on this darkest night.

With deep devotion to my wonderful father -Mridula

12. 'Human Life' -Entrust it a Purpose Profound

'Tick tick tick', she woke up hearing the sound,
Time slipping away from her grip, marking fate's
profound.
Yes, Time the decision maker runs out fast,
Writing everyone's story — of making or breaking at
last.

Time indeed never waits for anyone's mercy plea,
Yet courtesies roll in the same pace, impartial and free,
To poor and wealthy, men and women alike it flows,
To child and old, equanimous Time its rhythm knows.

She paused for a second, engrossed in thoughtful sway,
Am I making the best usage of my time each day?
To shape me, make me, build me and people around,
For that is the aim of my life — the divine purpose found.

To transform, to reform the world to a happier place,
To spread humanity's message — love, care with equal
face.
Equality, equanimity — core values we must hold,
Strengthening peace, justice, respect — our vigil's gold.

A world where rights blend with duties' sense of pride,
Smiles pervade each face, justice is the common stride.
Citizens access nature's resources with equal share,
Vigil in eyes, care in heart, sharing hands with
harmony's air.

Proud citizens engage in duty with self-respect's flame,
Mutual love, shared responsibility — India's noble name.
Live and let live, patriotism with security's embrace,
Persists for the old, mother, sisters — in full spirit, grace.

Wow, GREAT — a sense of GRATITUDE filled her heart,
To THE TIME GOD for instilling STRENGTH in her
mind's art.
A right direction to her foot's steady path,
A way from peril to vigil — gratitude's winning breath.

Thank you for winning over life's puzzle's maze,
A win over myself — aligning to virtue's timeless daze.
With vigilance awake, she vows to play her part,
In shaping a world where love, justice beat in every
heart.

With a vigilant usage of 'Time' for a profound cause-
Mridula

13."If Life Comes with an Expiry Date"

If birth comes with an "expiry date tag" inscribed,
Manmade things bear it — but life's timeline is whimsied.
Imagine a birth with a date far ahead, say 100 years vast,
Yet fear seeps in; the certainty of death breeds
uncertainty at last.

The thought that death is sure, looming swift and near,
Creates a tension — minutes flee, hours disappear.
Happiness trickles out, day by day's slow drain,
The thought paralyzes action; the spirit numbs without
passion's flame.

The waiting feels tedious, the end holds no surprise,
Whispers of death echo back, circling in restless mind's
skies.
The calendar taunts us; the stark fact stays the same,
Some await it resigned, some cry out for death's dark
frame.

Many yearn for release, some wish for life's extended
breath,
Time is God, Kalachakra wheels on with silent stealth.
It adjusts its own pace for those who dance with its flow,

"Ignorance is Bliss"let death come unannounced, let's
not know.

Let life be endless, happy in its own wild stint,
Feelings everlasting, relationships aglow like tint.
Let death arrive uninvited, sans a "save the date" note,
Let's savor endless life, boundless love, joy's infinite
vote.

Let Life unfurl fearlessly, unbound by waiting's tether,
Without a notice period, let its rhythm be wether.
Let's welcome it untagged, free from an "expiry date"
bind,
Embracing life's flow — timeless, limitless, passion left
unconfined.

with infinite Love - Mridula

14.Love is unconditional

Love is unconditional, pure and infinite grace,
Like Light, the Sun shines bright, wants nothing in
return's space.
Never sees the depth of darkness circling round,
Rises without flaw, unbounded, with radiant sound.
Unstoppable, never diminishing, never demanding a
claim,

Love is Like God's Blessings, showering with love's own
aim.
Always giving, not seeing who is receiving the flow,
Love is like the fragrance of a flower — spreading where
it grows.
Spreading around, not seeing who is near or afar in
sight,
Love is like the colour of a flower — enchanting beauty,
pure delight.
Beautifies without seeing anything dirty, low or high in
hue,

Love is like the softness of wool — gentle, touching
hearts anew.
Always feels the same way, it cools with tender care,
Love is like the breeze — roaming free with ease in

morning air.
Roams around with way it eases hearts and troubled
mind,
Love is like the Fire — engulfing with passion, leaving no
bind.

Love is like water — filling spaces, not seeing where it's
poured deep,
Not seeing worth or worthless, just flowing, love's own
secrets keep.
Love is like sea waves — touching any feet that lay
towards the shore with grace,
Gentle or fierce, love's touch reaches out, in every tender
place.
Love is like the sky — spreading its wings always high
and wide,
Embracing all beneath, no boundaries love does reside.

Oh men !you are destined to love unconditionally,
Let it be anyone around, let it flow like sound, wild and
free.

With unconditional Love- Mridula

15.My Mother-The Abode of Goodness

Oh Mother, I didn't realize the goodness you embodied,
Nor did I know this would be our last meeting.
I didn't know I'd never see this smiling face again,
Or bask in the warmth of your love.

Your gentle smile, which once lit up my world,
Will no longer bloom.
Your love, a boundless ocean,
Will no longer flow towards me.
Your strength, which stood by me, is now gone.

I had hoped to be forever enveloped in your love,
To bask in the warmth of your tender touch.
I wished to forever bask in the glow of your love,
And be blessed with your divine presence.

Your words were nectar, your love, a shelter.
I thought your presence would forever be by my side,
Your warm kisses, a constant solace.
But alas, I was mistaken.

My heart yearns for your love and tender touch.
I am left with memories of your kindness and care.

I know your hands will always protect me,
Your light will guide me, and your love will envelop me.

Oh Mother, I know you are always with me,
In my heart, in my thoughts, and in my soul.
I pray that God's blessings be upon you,
And that you are forever cherished and loved.

With unconditional love to Mother, the Abode of
Goodness-Mridula

16.The Wealth of Freedom

We chase the shadows, of a wealth unseen,
Buying things we don't need, to fit in the scene.
We wear the mask, of success and pride,
But true wealth lies hidden, deep inside.

It's not about the cars, or the mansion's might,
But freedom's call, that echoes through the night.
The freedom to choose, to live life our way,
To wake up when we want, and seize the day.

Money's a tool, to gain control and peace,
Not a means to impress, or our worth to release.
When we focus on freedom, we make wise choices too,
Saving, investing, and building assets anew.

The richest ones, aren't always on display,
They live life quietly, in their own way.
No need for validation, or a crowd to impress,
They've found the secret, to true happiness.

So let's not chase money, for attention's sake,
But for independence, and freedom's sake.
For when we own our time, and our lives are our own,
That's when we'll find, the wealth we've been seeking to

call home.

Aspiring for the Wealth of Freedom -Mridula

17.Patience -The Guide to Wisdom

Patience is the gentle rain that falls,
Nourishing the soul, and calming the walls.
It's the soft whisper that guides us through the night,
And leads us to the dawn, where love and peace take
flight.

Patience is the anchor that holds us fast,
The calm in every storm, the peace that will last.
It's the wisdom that guides us, through life's joys and
fears,
And helps us find the strength, to dry our tears.

So let's practice patience, and let our hearts be still,
And find the peace that comes from trusting in life's will.
For in patience, we find strength, and a sense of inner
peace,
A sense of connection to the universe, and a heart that's
released.

Love you all with Patience and Care-Mridula

18.A Mind So Sweet

When my mind is free from bitterness's stain,
I find the beauty, in life's joyous refrain.
No sorrow's shadow, no negativity's chill,
Just a heart that's light, and a spirit that's still.

In this sweet space, positivity blooms and thrives,
A garden of joy, where love and peace survive.
Every experience, a chance to grow and learn,
A mind that's nurtured, with kindness that yearns.

With a heart so light, and a soul so free,
I dance with life, in perfect harmony.
No weight of resentment, no burden to bear,
Just a sense of peace, that's always there.

In this sweet mind, love and compassion flow,
A sense of unity, with all that grows.
I'm connected to all, in a dance so fine,
A celebration of life, in all its design.

May my mind remain sweet, and my heart stay light,
A beacon of positivity, shining through the night.

Wishing You All A Sweet Mind - Mridula

19.Resilience -The Unbreakable Spirit

Resilience is the whisper of the soul,
A gentle reminder that we're whole.
It's the fire that burns, the flame that never fades,
A beacon of hope, in the darkest shades.

With every step, we rise above the pain,
And find the strength to carry on, to love again.
Resilience is the bridge that spans the gap,
Between despair and hope, between darkness and the map.

So let's stand tall, and face the test,
With resilience as our shield, and hope as our crest.
For we are stronger than we think, and capable of more than we know,
And with resilience, we'll rise above, and shine like the morning glow.

Building Resilience Every Moment -Mridula

20.Awake the Ram & Sita in us -The inner spark

In the digital haze, we wander astray,
Where loyalty's tested, and commitment's at play.
Kali Yuga's darkness, a prophecy now true,
Temptation's omnipresent, in all we view.

We normalize compromise, a subtle decay,
Principles are questioned, and values fade away.
But deep within, a spark remains,
A potential for greatness, a Ram-like refrain.

Sita's strength, a beacon in the night,
Guides us forward, a shining light.
We must awaken, and let our true selves show,
Conquer the 'Ravana' within, and let our virtues grow.

Let's not just burn effigies, a symbolic act,
But strive to vanquish our inner demons, and react.
With self-awareness, and a commitment strong,
We'll rise above the noise, and sing a different song.

In this age of compromise, let's stand tall,
With Ram-like fortitude, and Sita's gentle call.
For within us lies the power, to choose the right path,

And emerge victorious, in the battle of life's math.

Commiting to conquer the 'Ravana' within-Mridula

21.The Feminine Grace, the Essence of Womanhood

Woman is Shri, the embodiment of grace,
Prosperity and Lakshaving Lakshmi's divine glow.
She is Shakti, the power that sustains,
Without her, there's no life, no purpose that endures.

She is the soul of man, his guiding light,
Worshipping her is worshipping the self, a sacred rite.
It's worshipping the divine, a blessing from above,
Bringing prosperity, peace, and endless love.

They say she was born from man's rib, a myth to dispel,
For without her strength, humanity would falter and fell.
She's the creator, the nurturer, the one who sustains,
Her power is immense, her love that reigns.

In her absence, there's no progress, no growth, no might,
She's the foundation, the strength that holds tight.
When she's pleased, life's a joy, a sweet delight,
Her love is the melody that fills the night.

In her love, we find our peace, our soul's refrain,
The waves of her affection, a soothing balm that remains.
In her presence, life's transformed, pure and divine,

A reflection of her love, a beauty that's sublime.

In her light, our hearts find solace, our souls take flight,
In her love, we find our strength, our guiding light.
She's the essence of life, the rhythm and the beat,
A symphony of love, a dance that's sweet.

With the Divine Feminine Energy &Love Always-
Mridula

www.ingramcontent.com/pod-product-compliance
Lightning Source LLC
Chambersburg PA
CBHW050949030426
42339CB00007B/357